S U B M E R G E

Also by K.Y. Robinson
The Chaos of Longing

 Enjoy *Submerge* as an audiobook narrated by
the author, wherever audiobooks are sold.

SUBMERGE

K.Y. ROBINSON

Andrews McMeel
PUBLISHING®

Andrews McMeel Publishing
a division of Andrews McMeel Universal
1130 Walnut Street, Kansas City, Missouri 64106

www.andrewsmcmeel.com

19 20 21 22 23 BVG 10 9 8 7 6 5 4 3 2 1

ISBN: 978-1-5248-5065-4

Library of Congress Control Number: 2019943366

Editor: Melissa R. Zahorsky
Art Director: Holly Swayne
Production Editor: Dave Shaw
Production Manager: Cliff Koehler

Cover design by Iram Shahzadi
Interior illustrations by Angga Agustiya

Attention: Schools and Businesses

Andrews McMeel books are available at quantity discounts with bulk purchase for educational, business, or sales promotional use. For information, please e-mail the Andrews McMeel Publishing Special Sales Department: specialsales@amuniversal.com.

for the ocean inside of us.

CONTENTS

IMMERSE

sea of me

bondage and jubilee
hymns and broken hallelujahs
created the sea of me.

go to the water

pastor said to go to the water
to find my reflection in you.
cleanse my soiled soul.
to fill this overturned vessel.
to right this wrong.

when i arose, i felt empty.
your waves passed through me
and redemption felt so elusive.

letters

as i child i secretly read the letters my mama wrote to god. i unwrapped them and devoured every word like candy. i wanted to see him through her eyes. to shake the shroud of my skepticism and to know her better.

some letters were uplifting and full of wonder. others broke my heart. her faith quivered at times but remained on the surface. meanwhile my faith was submerged like stones at the bottom of the river gasping for air.

one day the letters were gone. did they find their way to god or did her faith sink to the bottom like mine?

riverside

i tried to lay down my burdens
but they clung to my sinful skin.

daydreams

as a child i daydreamed about living in a different world. a world where i couldn't hear gunshots ringing in the distance. a safe haven from the vultures circling when my body ripened before my mind. a house that wasn't ridden with rats and roaches.

i daydreamed about living in a big house with large windows that let in light even on the darkest of days. a backyard patio where i could watch the rain pitter-patter peacefully. a balcony that hovered near the moon. a garden of roses that never withered. a home filled with so much music and laughter i could burst.

as i got older the daydreams came to an end. i saw the magic my parents weaved whenever they made something out of nothing. i learned to count my blessings and stopped wishing for someone else's life.

formless (haiku)

the water inside
billowing and cascading
takes different shapes.

duality of water

a life-giving force
can become a life taker
with each swallowing wave.
this is the duality of water.

secrets

water carries many secrets
that are too heavy to tell.

it is a floating graveyard
for my ancestors'
burdened bones
on the ocean floor.

it will hold the weight
of your past sins
and carry them
out to sea.

it will engulf memories
to remind you that it
is vengeful and never
loses its memory.

at first sight

one day your heart is a stone.
callous and cold to the touch
but when your eyes meet
theirs for the first time,
you become an ocean.
waves inside you crash
and drench you in a thing
you're too afraid to name.

the first kiss (haiku)

our lips were waves
crashing into each other.
a safe place to drown.

first love

when i think of your love, i smell sandalwood and feel
the lull of lavender. honey fills my mouth. i hear birds
chirping to the rhythm of your laughter. i see the sun
surrounding you like a halo. i can feel waves ebbing and
flowing inside your chest when you pull me in the tide of
your arms. you overwhelm me when you touch me with
your hungry hands and make a meal of me. i've found
new universes in the unfolding nebulas of your eyes.
you are the first one my heart cracked open for. water
me until i'm in full bloom. fill every crevice. take me to a
place where love lives and never dies.

like water

i will always remember
to quench you
be your stillness
and pour myself
into you like water.

transcend

you reminded me of him, but you were softer with me
and the space you carried. you were a never-ending
bloom. i wanted to tiptoe inside your essence and inhale
and get lost in the sunflower field of you. we found our
way to an empty lecture hall. a raw desperation came
over us once the door slammed shut. we kissed as if
every unspoken word could be manifested through our
bodies. as if we could transcend to another dimension. as
if we were stars aching to become supernovas. i haven't
been kissed like that ever since.

swept away

i fell in love with you when
the rolling wave of your laugh
brought me peace.

when the indigo sea of your eyes
welcomed my wading,
no matter how clumsy i was.

when your hands felt like sunrise
over the cold horizon
i become sometimes.

fleeting

desire is fleeting.
it blooms and withers.
what is left after it rises
and collapses into itself
and leaves me in ruins?
i'd rather be anchored in love.

a flowering friendship

a true friend watches you bloom
and doesn't resent the sunlight.
prunes you when your growth is stagnant.
waters you when you feel like wilting.
and you never need to pluck petals
to question their love for you.

and it was so good
> after iain s. thomas

you opened a corner of my heart
and shined a light
and it was so good.

you drop-kicked my shell
and made it safe to crawl out
and it was so good.

you laced every room with love
every time you smiled
and it was so good.

you helped me clench
and bury the peach pit of my nerves
and it was so good.

i saw my soul reflected
in the river of yours
and it was so good.

homegirls

we embraced our differences. we walked into womanhood together. wiped away each other's tears. told harsh truths we didn't want to hear. nearly lost each other over something silly. went on ridiculous recon missions to catch cheating boyfriends. dropped it like it was hot and found it harder to pick it back up as we got older. laughed so hard it tore the roof off our grief. encouraged each other to grow. to move on. to take a chance on ourselves. i don't know where i would be without your love and guidance. you are my rock and a soft place to land.

ode to my toy friends

oh the mechanic miracles
that never break my heart
or ignore text messages.
to the things that buzz in the night
that aren't cicadas.

to the bullet killing the craving
in a dark alley between the sheets.
the rabbit hopping happily in my valley.
the wand and its magic tricks.
the butterfly pea blooming
from pressure waves.

to the tight-lipped joy
and rivers emptying from me.
they helped me gather my shame
and exhale it like smoke.
reminded me that this is my body
and the blood surging through it.

to make music of myself.
to summon every melody trapped
and become a song unhinged.
thank you.

submerge

i want to be water.
to inhabit over half
your body and earth.
to pivot between
quenching your thirst
and drowning you alive.

waves of longing

stretch me out
like an ocean.
slit my waves with
your lightning
and become cloudless
in your longing.

water me

come to me
in the night
drenched in longing
and my body
will crack open
from the thirst.

water me.
end the drought
loneliness
makes of me.
release the flood
you cannot contain.

not a love poem

collapse underneath
the velvet of me
as i unweave your desire.

fruit bowl

in my womb there are
flesh-filled plums,
an orange and grapefruit.
a bunch of bizarre spheres
unfit to eat
or press into wine.
this is how unruly
my garden grows.

i tried to pluck them
from the only home
they've ever known
but they returned
stubborn as weeds
choking my fertile
soil.

for nina simone

the trembling water
of your voice
is a baptism.

soluble

i search for water
in your mouth
to dissolve the salt
others left behind.

DROWN

our last kiss

i remember the last kiss
and how you pulled away
from me like a tide.

when they leave

i break every
bough in me
trying to make
the wrong ones
love me.
when they leave
i become
a brittle branch bare
swaying in the
breeze of ache
finding it hard
to replant myself
on solid ground.

gone

the night your nomadic love left
for greener pastures, my body
became a monument erected
on the hollow ground of your heart.

it commemorated every
touch, kiss and i love you.
your kaleidoscope of guilt
and my rose-colored denial.

i want to beg you to stay.
to not make stone of me.
to not visit me when you're
feeling nostalgic.
bring me back to life.
bring us back to life.

the sailor and the siren

you used to find refuge in me
but now you're swimming
against the current of us.

my desperation grows more teeth
trying to make you stay and
ripping the sinews of my heart.

she lured you with her siren song
and i haven't seen you since.
but i will gather your severed pieces
when you wash ashore.

oxbow

meander.
make clay of me.

break away.
isolate me on
my crescent-shaped
marsh of despair.

leave me to evaporate
as you make your way
to the other fishes
in the sea.

drowning in love

your name pooled inside me
and i swallowed every wave
to drown my love for you.

miracle

turn the saltwater
of your absence
into wine.

withered

the color of desire that
once flowered for us
has yellowed
and withered.
the water has left.
you've made
a desert of me.

the last time

i hope this is the last time.
i hope the ichor
of her name
has left your veins
and stops flooding
what we have built.

i hope the sand of
your time with her
is no longer
between your toes.
in our bed.
in your memory.

i hope i can
rest the corners
of my eyes
for once.

i hope my vessel
will be enough
even if it's still capsized
from the last time
you turned my world
upside down.

things changed

we broke promises
like driftwood
and used the fire
we made at night
to keep us warm.

honeypot

my heart is as eager as my mouth.
a tsunami lying in wait.
ready to engulf and mistake
the unimaginable for love.

i should've told you that
you would have to search
for higher ground.

i push you away
and pull you back in
with the one thing
you could never resist.

the way we were

i want to go back in time
when we were heavy with water.
when you pulled me into
the undertow of you
and overwhelmed me.
when the lather of longing
was enough to keep us afloat.

missing you

i miss bringing you into the fold of my body and
breathing you in. getting lost in your eyes. tracing my
fingers across your trembling body. getting drunk off
cheap liquor and each other. swaying in your arms as you
sing to me. i miss the way you called me *beautiful* and
made me believe it. watching bad movies just to make
fun of the silly story lines. i don't remember the last time
i laughed so hard and felt so safe in someone's arms.
sometimes i wonder if you ever miss me too.

chambers

i tried to find music
in the chambers of your heart
but every string snapped
and became trip wire.
i never thought loving you
would be an orchestra of ache.

ebbed

your body ebbed
away from mine
when i needed
water the most.
i wake up wading
in knee-deep ache
reaching for you
in the dark.

shoreline

you carry oceans
in your eyes
and won't let me
close enough
to swim in them
because you know
i would lose myself
and drown.

smoke and rot

i kept my ear to the ground
and inhaled the smoke
from your scorched heart.
i would rather smolder
in your arms to prove
i was there than leave
your ashes behind.

misplaced kisses

when you kissed me it felt like
you were searching for someone
who didn't exist and i let you because
i wanted to be anyone else but myself.

all the petty things i hope

there you go again—being happy without me. kissing her in the parking lot right outside my apartment like i don't have windows! i hope your lips turn into a swarm of bees and she recoils in horror. when you hold her hand, i hope cactus needles sprout. i hope you knock on my door to ask for tweezers. i'll pretend i'm not home even though you just saw me sneering through my blinds.

there you go again thinking she's the one. i hope every woman alive shape-shifts into her. all races, shapes and sizes. i hope they're mean to you. ask you to hold their purses at the same time. tell you to sleep outside like the dog you are. she'll no longer be the woman of your dreams but multiple versions of your nightmares.

i hope you knock on my door again. i'll still pretend i'm not home as i rub my hands together like an evil genius. i hope you slowly slide down my door and cry out that there's no one like me.

photograph

your smiles were
so big and bright
they rivaled the sun
and i became
the rueful raisin
shriveling inside
your happiness.

gary

you were my first crush and i would like to think that
you liked me too. one day after school we ducked down
in a back seat of the school bus and i gave you a quick
peck on the lips. our classmates screamed with laughter.
it was the talk of the third-grade town the next day.
i didn't mind. *gary is my boyfriend now* i thought to
myself. at lunchtime when someone asked you about me
you said that i was ugly and you didn't even know me.
this was when i learned that boys like you only wanted
girls like me in the shadows.

puppy love

mama tells me that he still loves me after all this time. that he waits for my return like a faithful dog—after two failed marriages and children. isn't it so convenient that his love sprouted for me when his garden became a ghost town?

she tells me that it is best when a man loves you more than you love him because he'll be endlessly devoted to you, but what if the love isn't there anymore?

at 14, everything about love was an iridescent fairy tale. i'm much older now and love has taken different shapes and colors. i've bloomed and withered. been bruised and mended. i don't see love as a never-ending summer anymore, but sometimes i wish i did.

humpty-dumpty heart

i asked you why you chose her instead of me. you said that some people are just meant to be friends. but you didn't kiss or touch me like a friend. you made me rise from my body like a ghost. kissed me with so much desperation that it left me breathless.

now you're gone and won't reply to my messages. but i know it won't last. it never does. you always come back disassembled at my door waiting for me to put your humpty-dumpty heart back together again. to kiss her away too. to be your *break glass in case of emergency heartbreak* body. and i let you break it like a fucking fool.

the last time i saw you

the last time i saw you,
you cupped my face
like you were trying
to fill it with love,
but i cracked underneath you.
i don't know how to be full
without overstuffing myself.

i have a girlfriend

i hadn't heard from you in weeks and wondered why
i didn't exist to you anymore. one lonely night i asked
to come over. i wanted you to remember my amber
perfume invading your senses. my sternum heaving
toward the heavens as you explored the meridians of my
body. i needed you to mend the gutted fish my heart had
become when you tossed me back into the sea.

when i entered, the air was different. it felt like i didn't
deserve to breathe it anymore. your mouth was a distant
sea, but i still hoped your lips would sail toward mine.
i touched you, but you didn't tremble. i spelled out my
desire, but you were too distracted to decipher it.

you paid more attention to your phone than usual. when
you received a message your face lit up like a jar of
fireflies. i wanted to know who was the magician who
could touch you without being in the same room. i finally
took the hint and left. i cried myself to sleep and never
contacted you again.

a few months later i ran into you when my car was
stalled in traffic. i began to cry because you were the
only one who stopped even though you didn't know
anything about cars. you sat with me as i waited for the
tow truck. you apologized for your behavior and said *i
have a girlfriend and it's getting serious. we're looking for
a house.*

my heart collapsed under the weight of the love you will never give me. you showed me a picture of her and i memorized everything about her and made comparisons inside my head. you gushed on and on about her, but i didn't stop you—even when the light in your eyes brought tears to mine.

i forced a smile and said *i'm so happy for you.* the tears eventually turned into laughter as we caught up on old times. in that moment i was grateful that i wasn't alone in a busy intersection in the texas heat. when you left, you said *i love you sweetie* but all i heard was *i found someone better.*

the girl of your dreams

she doesn't have to carry
an ocean between her thighs
for you to wade in
until you're drenched in salt.

she doesn't need
a monsoon mouth
to engulf and
swallow you whole.

she makes you happier
in ways i never could
without using her body
and losing herself.

the sailors

the one with the aquamarine eyes said
the objects he floated in my sea
were smaller than they appeared.
i parted myself until
i was emptied of salt,
so he could swim
in his fantasy of me.

the one with the sinewy hair
found treasures
locked inside me
but later claimed
i meant nothing to him—
only debris on the ocean floor
of his desire.

the one with the tree trunk arms said
my heart became
too heavy to carry.
that i should leave it
in a mason jar
before he came over.

the one with the wandering eyes
memorized every ripple
my body made for him
and used it against me
until it felt unholy.

the one with the seafoam eyes
disappeared for months at a time
when he became brackish
to my touch.
i knew he would return because
salt made the body
more tender for the taking.

sandcastles

an ocean of men made
sandcastles of me
and washed me away
with their waves
after their longing receded.

false alarm

the waves of nostalgia
overwhelmed me.
i smelled salt in the air
and mistook it for you
coming back.

playing catch up

i'm still learning how to let you go but i find myself
looking in the rearview of my memories. perhaps a part
of me is hoping your heart will catch up to mine.

sail away

you said to come closer. that it felt like there was an
ocean between us. you were right. i placed it on my back
and strapped it there. i'm so used to everyone leaving, so
i decided to sail away first. to keep my heart inside my
chest. it's not as buoyant as it used to be.

loneliness (haiku)

my loneliness is
a wildfire in need of
a water bearer.

emotional laborer

i summoned honey
to quench bitter veins,
until my honeycomb melted.

fermented

i ran away from home. met him on a bus. ran out of food.
called him. went to his place. he plucked, washed and
peeled my fruit without consent. placed it in the stockpot
of power and perversion. he brought me to a boil. i
dissolved into myself just the way he wanted. he mashed
me until i was the consistency of applesauce. until i
no longer recognized myself. allowed me to cool. to
dissociate. to stare blankly at the ceiling. he poked small
holes in the plastic wrap of my innocence—allowing me
to breathe but not to speak. laid me to rest to become a
ghost of a girl. i contemplated resurrection. he skimmed
off the rest of me floating at the surface before leaving
for work. i called my parents. the secret stayed sealed
inside my vessel for years. i've learned that there are
things water cannot cleanse no matter how hard you try
to scrub them away.

the haunting

tell me what to do with the rot because
there are times trauma summons
the ghosts of men that haunt me
and i'm taken back kicking
and screaming as they rake me over
the hot coals of my memories.

reputation

when the neighborhood boys gave me an ounce of attention, i gave my body to them. i mistook their desire for love because i didn't love myself. when those same boys whispered about me the next day, i wanted to disappear to a distant galaxy. when the rumors found their way to my parents' porch, my father solemnly carried the shame. it simmered underneath his eyes when he looked at me but he spared me his wrath. my mother was the opposite. she swung the shame from every room from dusk to dawn and sliced me with the knife-edge of her words. i felt like a stain they wished they could wash away. i tried to disappear three times, but even the galaxy wouldn't take me.

**to the black women and femmes seen as trees and
not flowers**

everyone expects you to be a tree.
to bloom without sunlight and water.
to be anything but a flower.
to be only visible for your resilience
and the fruit you bear.

to withstand carvers confessing
their love for everyone else but you.
to drain your sap
for their consumption.

to cut yourself open
so they can count the rings
of joy and sorrow boiling
in your bloodline.

to survive the elements
society throws at you
without dirtying its hands
or knees to tend to your roots
because you were built for this.

river running red

the timeline is flooding again. another black body has become a river running red on the pavement. a black mother will soon wade in grief on the edge of her son's river. when a hashtag is born, a black angel gains their wings. i think of my nephew and how his kind eyes and shy smile matter less than the color of his skin. i think of my middle-aged disabled brother who cannot understand simple commands. i think of the men i've loved with bayou brown eyes and burnt umber skin. i think of all shades seen as menace before human. i think of my niece and how her big heart enters the room before she does. i wonder if it will startle someone someday. i think of how i steady my breath when a police car follows me for several blocks before turning around.

tropical storm allison

floodwaters rushed through
the ghetto and engulfed what
we struggled to get.

floorboards uprooted themselves.
mold crawled up the walls.
memories were washed away.

i searched for my poems
in piles of muddy water
and came up empty.

we stayed in a fume-filled
fema trailer for months.

my father rebuilt our little home
and it slowly came back to life.

hurricane ike

i was home alone and terrified. the wind howled like
a freight train haunted by ghosts. trees stretched and
slapped their limbs against my window with fury. i made
the hasty decision to leave in the midst of the hurricane.
the rain and wind violently swirled around me like
ribbons as i made my way to my car. i felt my car pushing
as i drove down the dark desolate street. suddenly, a
flash of light illuminated a fallen tree i nearly crashed into
head-on. i drove home and hid in my closet until the next
morning. that night, i learned you have to ride out the
storm and not succumb to it.

hurricane harvey i

my mother and brother fled their home when the water began to rise. she underestimated the water's depth and had to escape the car before it was swept away. they made their way to a convenience store and eventually an overpass as the water rose higher and higher.

a boat passed by but never came back for them. she took shelter with a small group of people who were known to engage in unbecoming behavior in the neighborhood but at that moment it was about survival. her shoes floated away and as a diabetic she feared she would cut her feet in the contaminated water. my brother could barely walk at that point. they stayed the night in an abandoned apartment, but she was terrified the entire time and hardly slept.

when she finally called me, i was relieved but felt guilty for being safe. i told her to call the cops, but the looters she was with—who feared being prosecuted—forbade her. on the third day, she and my brother arrived at my uncle's and were clothed and fed. once the roads were cleared, i took them to my place and they lived with me for several months. when i think of survival and strength, i think of my mother. she lost everything twice and saved herself and my brother, overcoming the weight of water.

hurricane harvey ii

harvey hollowed out my mother's home and heart like
a seashell. she was mourning the loss of my father more
than ever. i watched the *he would know what to do* and
he took care of everything sweep across her face.

grief quietly flooded the room and we sat in silence. i
held the levee against my tears. this wasn't the time for
them. my father would suck his teeth from beyond the
grave if i cried in that moment.

i filled out the confusing paperwork, contacted insurance
and government agencies and researched home
rebuilders. i never knew how exhausting the process
would be. later that night i released my tears while
everyone slept. i think she did too. the water wasn't done
with us yet.

on losing my father

every wave
inside me
wailed when you
left this earth
and i never learned
the art of floating.

how are you?

i'm fine.[1]

---

[1] i am not fine. i'm drowning in my thoughts. i cried myself to sleep last night and it took everything in me just to get out of bed this morning. i'm exhausted. i feel hopeless and alone. i feel like no one understands. help me. help me. help me.

murky

i haven't left the house, brushed my teeth, washed my body or the dishes in days. clothes are cowering in the corner. the fridge is as empty as i am. take-out containers and bottles are tossed on the floor. *i'll do it tomorrow* i tell myself but sometimes i don't want tomorrow to come. sometimes the world becomes a murky sea and i can't see myself in it.

the last episode

you broke up with me after three years. you said i was crazy and needed help. i didn't want it to be over. i needed to convince you to love me again and that i would scrape out the last dollop of my sanity and place it on a platter for you if it meant i could keep you.

i tearfully took the two-hour bus ride to your place. i waited by your door like a stray animal hoping to find scraps of us to nibble on, something to sustain me until you returned for me.

then something inside of me snapped like a weathered branch and uprooted me from reality. i had never seen that side of me before. my depression turned into a category 4 hurricane. it destroyed and flooded everything in its path.

you said you would've killed me if you had caught me in the midst of my manic storm. you didn't have the compassion and patience to deal with my monsters anymore. they finally scared you away for good.

72-hour hold

my mother urged me to seek professional help. she said i'd always carried a tsunami of sadness, even as a child. but lately it had morphed into something else. she was right. i didn't even recognize myself. i was nervous, irritable and wanted a way out of my skin. after seeing the doctor at a clinic, he urged immediate hospitalization. my days at the facility were a blur. all i can remember is how cold it was. and meeting with a doctor in a gated room during the day. and a man screaming. although there was a name to what i was feeling, i was more confused than ever. was i broken? would it be like this forever? what now?

everyday struggle

there are two people
living inside of me.
a tug of war of the mind.
there are days i'm
a dancing dolphin
and bloodthirsty shark.
as full as the ocean
and empty as a seashell.
a tranquil current
and a rogue wave
of devastation.

who will i be today?

end of euphoria

it got a hold on me
and i danced for hours.
every beat reverberated
through my body
and became my new blood.

i didn't want it to leave.
it made me feel like i held
the universe in the
pools of my irises and
in the bends of my body.

then the dark side
of the moon came.
i burned myself out like a star
and crashed into melancholy.

the marmalade of mania
was no longer sticky and sweet.
my mind turned against me.

isolation

i isolate myself
and become a tree
so no one can hear
when my mind
splits itself open,
strips the bark
of my façade,
ransacks the terrain
and makes me a wasteland.

in my mind

my mind is a train of thoughts racing and derailing until i'm standing in a fog of forgetfulness.

my mood swings from every branch, high and low. sometimes the branches snap and i land face-first into a puddle of mud. sometimes i reach the heavens.

i become a conveyor belt of creativity and productivity and feel useless when the factory shuts down.

i chase the mania before it leaves town because i know depression is around the corner and i can't shake myself dry once it has drenched me.

i drown in crying spells i didn't cast.

i go off my meds because i feel like a zombie or when i foolishly feel cured.

i use sleep as an escape or escape sleep when i'm feeling restless.

i ache to be planted and uprooted from the earth.

being bipolar is like riding a roller coaster against my will.

no one understands

i can't talk about my mental illness without feeling like a
burden. without being reminded that insurance policies
do not pay out for suicides. that i should drop to my
knees and pray away the demon of depression. that my
lack of faith is the cause for the chaos in my mind.

they want to know why i'm depressed. most of the
time there isn't a specific reason. there are times i wake
up irritated and withdrawn, so depressed that i want
everything around me to burn to the ground. other times
i could wake up brighter than a sunbeam and end up an
eclipse right before their eyes.

they think i shouldn't be depressed because my dreams
came true but mental illness doesn't pack its bags and
leave because good things are happening.

they say it could be worse, but this is my worse. my
mental illness is a foreign language that i'm tired of
translating. it's exhausting trying to balance my chemical
imbalance on the tightrope of their assumptions.

how do i explain these feelings to people who have never
experienced them before but who try to invalidate my
illness at every single turn?

what to say on your online dating profile

the article said to sound like you're down-to-earth. to make playful fun of yourself. to be creative. well, my mania dances until it spins off its top and some days my down-to-earth feels like i'm beneath the earth. my depression is an asteroid. it turns me into a crushed city that no one wants to visit but i will rebuild myself if you're into witnessing miracles. i've had more medications than serious romantic relationships. i'm still trying to find the right dosage and the right one. see, i know how to make playful fun of myself.

are you swiping right or picking me up at 8?

i'm afraid you'll leave

i'm afraid you'll find out
i'm not the tropical escape
i was last night.
i let you leave
as soon as you're done
so you won't see my daylight
morph into midnight
in all its melancholy.

the weight of it all

it feels too heavy
to rise from bed
and draw back
the curtains
when the world sits
like a cinder block
pressed against
my rib cage.

to rehearse a smile
for the half-hearted
audience inside myself.

to take a shower
without wishing to
sink down the drain.

to feel the splintering sunlight
without wanting to shrivel
inside of it.

to clean my apartment.
to answer the phone.
to write this poem.

happy pills

my antipsychotics are a pink sky.
will they bend the light
and scatter away the darkness?

my antidepressants are aquamarine.
will they help me swim out this sea of sadness?

will they make my life a beach?

changing states

dark days drinking wine
until it tastes like water.
proving i can reverse a miracle.

listening to music to fill
the empty basin i've become.

free-falling into a deluge of desires
until i'm drenched and stranded
on my isle of regret.

questions for the mania

do you know
how to be full
without their tongues
becoming waves
to disappear into?

why do you build
a city of thoughts
in your head and turn them
against each other?

how do you make
money disappear
like a magic trick?

why is every
color so loud
that you could touch
and taste it?

half-past-midnight manic cleaning spree

it's half past midnight and i can't sleep. this place is filthy.
i have so much energy. i never have this much energy.
must make use of it. cleanliness is next to godliness.
maybe it'll make me a believer. i'm feeling really inspired
to reinvent myself. rid myself of worldly possessions. i'll
gather a mountain of clothes. toss them to the sea. may
the mermaids and sirens wear them well. strangle the
water from the mop and make it kiss the floor hard like
they do in the movies. the way i want to be kissed. get
on my hands and knees, exorcise the dirt and make the
vacuum scream as it swallows the filth. in the end i will
be drenched in sweat and triumphant.

dear depression

dear depression
you are a swallowed island.
a continental shelf of grief.
an underwater prison.
a fog holding the sky hostage
and chasing away the blue.
the sand is sludge.
the rain is constant
and nothing ever grows.
the head of palm trees
mourn the memory
of a sun that never rises.
the moon hides
the stars behind it.

i want to remember
what the sun feels like.
how warmly the sand kisses my feet.
i want to be anywhere but here
but no one believes me.
they think i should snap out of it.

depression nap

i flee to my bed
when i need to escape
the heaviness of the world.
to shove the sadness
between my sheets
weigh it down
with my blanket
to suffocate it
and hope it never returns.

as i lay lonely

late one summer night, the drumming in my chest
became so thunderous that it rattled my rib cage. my
breath became a shallow wind i couldn't catch. i thought
i was dying. i've wanted to die many times, but this
wasn't one of them.

so many thoughts went through my mind. what if the
article my best friend sent me the other day would
become my fate? what if i died alone and my body
wouldn't be discovered for days?

i thought about how no one was there to hold my hand.
not the men who never stayed long enough for pillow
talk. the people who had fuller lives than mine. the ones
who didn't need me until they needed something.

drenched in sweat i crawled outside and called 9-1-1. i
lay in my doorway like shattered glass. i hoped someone
would see me. if i was dying, i didn't want to do it alone.

the medics arrived and performed an ekg. my heart rate
was 160 beats per minute. they said i was experiencing
a panic attack and would be ok. i didn't believe them. i
tearfully begged them to take me to the hospital. that i
didn't want to die alone. in reality i think i didn't want to
be alone.

an hour and a lap full of vomit later, i was released from
the hospital. the nurse advised against calling a cab in
my state. i thumbed through the contacts on my phone
several times.

it was 1:00 a.m. there wasn't anyone i could call without feeling like a burden or overstepping my boundaries. the loneliness began to echo again. i caught an uber home. it was a lonely car ride to an even lonelier apartment.

i'm sorry

i want to sink into the horizon of my guilt when you
worry. when your heart collapses to your stomach when
i don't answer your calls. when you search for signs of
duress whenever we speak. when you wonder if i've
taken my meds. when you tread lightly so you won't
trigger me. i know you worry about me and i'm sorry.

how to go to group therapy

i. sit in the parking lot for several minutes
    until you swallow the lump stalled in your throat.

ii. gather your courage like freshly washed clothes. enter
    the room and pretend it isn't too heavy to carry.

iii. engage in awkward conversations until the session
     starts.

iv. feel the lump return when you're asked to introduce
    yourself. feel the urge to shrink but somehow rise out
    of it.

v. strip down your past and lay it bare. hear the
    room fall silent as they hang on every word like a
    precipice.

the symptom no one talks about

my veins feel electric.
i'm dahlia in my desire
ready to be plucked.

i'm fire-engine red.
sirens blaring.
a forest fire in need
of more kindling.
come to me with all the air
your mouth can carry
and cedar on your body.

you don't have to find me beautiful
or say that you love me.
we both know you never will.
let my body be the conduit
for the woman of your dreams.

why summon god
when i can bring you to your knees?
why fear the devil
when my body is both
fire and brimstone?

dear (redacted) and others i may have disappointed

i caved in to my compulsions.
became a map traced
by too many fingers.
the bodies are a blur.
you're all i see now.
salt the gaping wound.
wrap my wandering lust in thorns.
call me unholy.
tame the beast that boiled
and spilled between their sheets.
i promise to be good
and worthier of your love.

war of mind

i lose days at a time.
they pass through
me like water
until everything around me
is in drought.

EMERGE

water

harden and soften me.
flood and quench me.
break me like a levee
and take the shape
of my heart.
this is healing
from the bottom up.

when i realized it was over

i. your heart stopped sailing toward mine and left the shore.

ii. i became a tattered flag from surrendering to you time and time again.

iii. your mouth became an evaporated river every time i pressed my lips against it.

iv. my heart became a collapsed seawall from all the tears i cried.

v. there were no more lulls between our waves—only chaos.

smile for what?

you don't have to smile more.
to be softer than kneaded dough
for their rough hands.
your fire will never be too much.
rise and speak your mind
even if it burns.

not your mule

when they never ask about your day and always lay their
acres of hurt across your back you tell them you're not
their beast of burden. you battle wars every day and
there is no room for them or anyone else to grind your
good bones into dust.

this is who i am

my eyes are a message in a bottle
that has been broken by many
but i keep looking for good in everyone.

my seashelled heart has washed up
on every shore it tried to reach
but it keeps on beating.

my body swells like the ocean
and my voice is a timid wave
but i'm learning to embrace every curve
and speak up more.

i've sunk more ships than i've launched
but i'm learning to navigate the seas
without losing myself to the sailors.

tapestry

i used to burrow through
my bag of bitterness.
pull you out like twine.
poke my needle through
the frayed fabric of us.
unweave the ways
you never loved me.
re-stitch where it went wrong.
pinpoint why you left.
i was breaking my heart a second time
trying to find out why you broke it first.

waited and waited

i kneeled on the raw rice of our love and waited for water to overtake us. for you to be softer. searched for signs to prove the other signs wrong so i could stay lost in you. held the endless midnight of your heart in my hands and waited for the sun to rise. learned how to arch my back and adjust my eyes to the darkness. convinced myself that it was enough. tried to mend the broken shells inside of you until i became hollow. one day i grew tired of waiting for you. i finally felt the warmth of the sun and wrote my name in the sand without you. i didn't need you to be happy.

famine for love

i felt uninvited to love.
i stood on the outside
looking in like a ghost
and never the guest of honor.
i was led through the back doors
of lust after everyone left.
like a shameless rodent,
i devoured scraps of broken men
hoping it would fill me
but their bones rattled
inside my stomach.
their bodies couldn't cure
the famine spreading inside my heart.

i had to learn to be full without them.
to stop mistaking their bones for wind chimes.
there was music inside me all along.
i had to search within and listen.

why i write

i write about trauma and mental illness not to romanticize them. i write to lift the veil and give them a voice. to banish what's bottled up inside. to let light flood the exposed cracks. to strip away the shame. to honor every part of myself that i thought was dishonorable.

i write for people who swallowed stigmas and regurgitated them in time to save themselves. made themselves rest stops to keep the lonely from howling at the moon inside their chests. found it hard to love themselves when others couldn't. blamed themselves for the beasts that feasted on them. and persevered in spite of everything trying to tear them apart.

sanctuary

poetry is my sanctuary. it's a place where i can unweave
whatever is tangled inside of me, even when it hurts.

mausoleum of mistakes

i shrunk myself to become
a drop in their oceans.

drifted down to unknown parts
and further away from myself.

loved hearts that escaped
through my hands like sand.

succumbed to the sea of sadness
when they sailed away.

i did the unthinkable
for the want of water.

a gentle reminder

you are not wasted stardust.
do not collapse into yourself.

gratitude

count your blessings. if the list feels too short, repeat it
over and over until your mouth overflows with gratitude.

fight

there will be days when you won't be able to shake the salt of sadness from your skin. days when you'll want to be swallowed whole by the sky and sent to a place where pain is a distant memory.

depression will feed you lies. it will tell you that you're worthless, unlovable, a burden without a purpose.

do not listen to the lies. there is light on the other side. hold on.

it may not seem like it but

there is hope
there is hope.
there is hope.
there is hope.
there is hope.
there is hope.
there is hope.
there is hope.
there is hope.
there is hope.
there is hope.
there is hope.
there is hope.
there is hope.
there is hope.
there is hope.
there is hope.
there is hope.
there is hope.
there is hope.
there is hope.
there is hope.
there is hope.
there is hope.
there is hope.
there is hope.
there is hope.
there is hope.
there is hope.
there is hope.
there is hope.
there is hope.

a honey-filled life

life won't always
feel like saltwater
filling every crack
and crevice.
it will flood
with sweetness too.

sea of stigma

there are people swimming in the sea of stigma.
some would rather drown than be seen as a great white
shark—a danger to distance yourself from.

some keep their heads above water to breathe but don't
speak up.

they all share the same silence that makes them sicker—
the desire to drown or remain thirsty.

they need to feel safe enough to emerge.

let them.

waves of my mind

you want the chaos to subside
but you cannot manipulate
the swelling waves of my mind.
believe me, i've tried becoming
a waxing and waning moon
until i've fallen off my axis.

you can't erase that part of me
by pushing back the waves of my hair
to the shore of my neck.
parting me like a sea and diving in.
the antidote isn't you
but that didn't stop us from trying.

wasted times

i wasted many years ignoring the call of the waves and breaking the dawn in half with my hands. that ends today.

the cycle

i screamed
into the void.
into my pillows.
in the shower.
in places where
no one could hear me.

i barricaded
open wounds
behind my smile.
painted on
a brave face
and hurried home
to wash it off.

i've received
and rejected help.
stockpiled pills
in a shoebox
for my exit route
and flushed them
down the toilet.
i decided to live.

the talk

at the table we talked about the breakdown of a mind.
how self-medicating in unhealthy ways wasn't the answer.
it had been years since i'd talked to someone or taken
medication. the pills made me feel like a plant sitting in
a dark corner. deprived of water and sunlight. it was a
numbness that failed to transmute into happiness.

i thought it was better to feel everything than nothing
at all. to grasp the glitter of mania and crawl out of the
dark tunnel of depression. but the crash in the end wasn't
worth it anymore.

i wanted to cry until i became a puddle on the floor, but
something about you calmed me. it was the first time i
felt understood. it motivated me to make an appointment.

thank you.

what not to say to someone with mental illness

"it will pass."
mental illness is not a season. we deal with it daily.

"snap out of it."
mental illness is not a switch you can turn on and off.

"get out and smell the roses."
roses don't smell so sweet and the sun doesn't shine as
bright when the world is rotting around us.

"you don't look depressed."
many of us dress our depression in the finest of linens
and disrobe it in the shadows of our minds.

practice mindfulness with your words. they have the
power to build bridges or burn them to the ground.

what they should've said

"your life means something to me."

"i won't pretend to understand your pain,
but i'm here for you."

"what do you need in this moment?"

"i'm just a phone call away."

"you are not a burden."

"i love you."

"you are not alone."

hem of joy

i wonder if i'll ever touch
the hem of joy when my heart
is used to being woven in pain.

when i water my wounds
to remain rooted in the past.

when i enjoy exhuming graves
to find new bones to blame.

when i embrace ache
like an old friend
instead of realizing it has
overstayed its welcome.

when i house the hurt
as if the creaking doors
and cluttered rooms could
somehow bring me peace.

i want to shed
this part of myself
and unravel the resentment
to mend the tattered hem of my heart.

one day (reprise)

i will become
a river of light
carrying darkness
out to sea.

i will peel the husk
of my insecurities,
soak them in saltwater
and lay them to rest.

i owe this to myself.

tonight

i'm not a crushed city or a manic metropolis. i'm a calm sea. a squawking seagull in the distance. a pink-and-white sky. at home with myself.

stuff broken hearts do before they heal

fight sleep.
deny everything.
have one last cry.
call them every unholy name.
forgive the unforgivable.
lie in surrender
with bated breath
and parted thighs.
fear loving again.

forgiveness

i must crawl out of resentment
to forgive you but my body tenses
at the thought of releasing your sins
like a balloon.

they are not a balloon.
they are a wrecking ball that won't stop
swinging my way.

you make me want to curse the sky.
turn my hands into gallows
and strangle the sunlight.
snuff out the moon.
gather every star and
throw them to the lions.

i'm so used to storing my anger
in the undercarriage of my heart,
waiting for the right time to unleash it.
but i find myself buried in memories
that you have long forgotten.

how to write a happy poem

drench it in
the lacquer
of laughter.
feed it light.
make it blossom
away from the corner
where you once
hid yourself.

alignment

the dreams i thought
were buried in sorrowful soil
sprouted like a wild garden
and wrapped around me like a prayer.

find the lesson

when the waves of regret wash over you, do not get swept away. forgive yourself. make amends. find the lesson and search for higher ground.

wet and wild

you loved me, and i let it slip through my fingers because
it was too wet, all-consuming, and too grounded in
expectation. i'm sorry i treated your love like it was
too heavy to carry. i didn't know how to carry love for
myself.

i wanted to be free and wild as water. to quell droughts
and break the levee of my longings for whoever would let
me flood them.

i made it back to the shore and you were gone. i hope
you've found a love that isn't a floundering fish like mine.
a love that knows how to stand still and wade in the
vastness of you.

shipwreck

i no longer wait for the sea
to whisper your waves back to me
or wake up the sleeping seashells
and ask if they've kissed your feet.
i've pulled out the sunken anchor of my heart
and stopped grieving the shipwreck of us.

evaporate

one day your name will not
absorb in me like water.

i will stop planting seeds
in the cracked land
of your heart waiting
for love to blossom.

oceans will not flood
in the folds of my eyes
and carry me
outside of myself.

one day i will not break
when memories roll
like thunder.
i will fight the deluge
and pack my heart with sand.

it's too late

you returned like
a prodigal lover
on your knees with
salt on your skin.

i wanted to part myself
like the sea
i became for you
so many times.

to wade in your welcome.
to let you kiss every scar
you left behind.

i waited for this day:
for you to have eyes
for only me and search
for me outside the dark.

to tear away your armor
and let the flowers
in your rib cage bloom
but i've run out
of water for you.

ashes

when i transition, scatter my ashes in the sea. i want to
be one with my ancestors. i've spent enough time being
buried in my waking life. i don't want religiosity at the
ceremony. i've never been down with dogma. play or sing
my favorite songs. eat my favorite foods. i want laughter
to fill in the gaps where grief has made a home. i want
there to be an avalanche of *i love yous*. invite the man
i never stopped loving no matter how much you don't
want to invite him. i hope he recites a poem in a soft
low voice or shares his favorite memory of me. my last
request is for you not to carry so much of the loss that
you get swept away in the grief. move forward. live the
vibrant and joyful life i've always wanted you to live and
come back to the beach and tell me all about it.

my silent prayer

reverse the erosion
settling in my heart.
distill the saltwater.
make my heart pure
so i can love again
without fear,
overflowing
and losing myself.

dried flowers

softness doesn't reside
between us anymore.
i can't water thorns
and expect petals
to bloom in their place.
all i can do is press you
between these pages
and move on.

water yourself

when they siphon their love and leave, remember the ocean you carry inside you. remember that you are vast in all of your wonder. no one can take that from you no matter how much they try to empty you.

blossom

i was in full bloom before you
entered my garden and
will continue to blossom
long after you've stopped watering me.

weightless

i want a love
that feels weightless
in the thick of it all.
a hopeful horizon
to stretch my arms out to.
a love that never leaves
me empty handed.

emerge

there will be days when you'll feel
like you're floating
beneath the waves of healing
trying to claw your way
back to the surface.

days when you'll feel like
you're drifting
in a sea of doubt.

days when you'll feel
like you're screaming
underwater trying
to find your voice.

keep swimming.
never stop trying
to find your way.

let every wave crash
against your voice.
you command your sea.

the grit of healing

there are no paved roads
to healing.

you must build one
brick by brick.

there will be backtracks
before breakthroughs but—

you must collapse
into yourself
before rebuilding.

you must unearth
every wound
before learning
the power of salt.

you will build
that yellow brick road—

in your own time and
on your own terms.

sea glass

think of healing as becoming sea glass. there are
things in life that will leave you shattered. you will feel
discarded and rough around the edges. you may lose
what makes you soft. when the tides of life toss you
around, learn to be shaped by the highs and lows. you
will emerge weathered but wiser. the waves will always
carry you back to yourself.

upon further investigation

i am enough.
i am grateful for this life
no matter how much i've suffered
in my body, mind and soul.

i will keep fighting.
i will keep fighting.
i will keep fighting.

INDEX

acknowledgments

To my loved ones, thank you for being there for the dark times and the ones drenched in light.

I am eternally grateful to my editor, Melissa Zahorsky, my publisher, Kirsty Melville, and Andrews McMeel Publishing. Thank you for believing in my art and giving my books a home. It has been a life-changing experience!

I want to thank my poetry family for their encouragement, advice, and support. Words aren't enough to express how much I admire and respect you Amanda Lovelace, Cyrus Parker, Gretchen Gomez, Caitlyn Siehl, Iain S. Thomas, Nikita Gill, Trista Mateer, and Pierre Alex Jeanty. I wish I could list everyone I've met along the way, but please know that you are appreciated.

A special thank-you to the readers. I would not be here without you holding a space in your hearts and bookshelves for me. I'm forever grateful. Thank you. Thank you. Thank you.

about the author

K.Y. Robinson is an introverted writer based in Houston, Texas. She received a B.A. in journalism and M.A. in history from Texas Southern University. She has loved words pressed against pages since childhood and has been chasing them ever since.

Robinson draws from personal experiences as a woman of color and trauma and mental illness survivor. She is the author of *The Chaos of Longing* and *Submerge*.

www.kyrobinson.com

instagram: @iamkyrobinson
twitter: @iamkyrobinson